Shots

First published in 2012 by
New Holland Publishers
London • Sydney • Cape Town • Auckland
www.newhollandpublishers.com

Garfield House 86–88 Edgware Road London W2 2EA United Kingdom
1/66 Gibbes Street Chatswood NSW 2067 Australia
Wembley Square First Floor Solan Street Gardens Cape Town 8001 South Africa
218 Lake Road Northcote Auckland New Zealand

ISBN: 9781742572383

Publisher: Fiona Schultz
Publishing manager: Lliane Clarke
Senior editor: Mary Trewby
Cover designer: Kimberley Pearce
Production manager: Olga Dementiev
Printer: Toppan Leefung Printing Limited

10 9 8 7 6 5 4 3 2 1

Follow New Holland Publishers on
Facebook: www.facebook.com/NewHollandPublishers

Shots

Little drinks to get the party started

Steve Quirk

NEW HOLLAND

CONTENTS

Introduction

This book has been designed for the purpose of providing an extensive range of shooters (shots) from basic mixers through to exotic creations. It demonstrates that there is nothing complicated about preparing and constructing a shooter. With 200 shooter recipes at your finger tips to select from, you will never be short of a shooter recipe or two.

Your answers to questions such as: How to chill a glass? How to frost a glass? How to layer ingredients? And what bar equipment is required? All these answers are provided in the introduction of this book.

Approximate % alcohol volume (% alc/vol) content has been calculated and supplied for each shooter in this book, as well as how many standard drinks each contains.

These calculations are based on information obtained that is believed to be accurate and reliable, although cannot be guaranteed due to % alc/vol variations between the different brands of spirits and liqueurs. These calculations should only be used as a guide.

The % alc/vol for all spirits and liqueurs required for shooters contained within this book are provided in the glossary – if unsure then compare your spirits and liqueurs with the % alc/vol provided in the glossary.

Constructing a Shooter

Shaking – When ingredients are required to be shaken, half fill a cocktail shaker with ice, and then pour ingredients into shaker over the ice. This will chill the ingredients quicker than pouring the ingredients into shaker before ice. Avoid over-filling your shaker – leave room for shaking. To shake, stand still and shake vigorously for about ten seconds, strain into chosen glass and serve or garnish. The majority of cocktail shakers have a strainer; if yours does not then you can use a hawthorn strainer. Effervescent drinks should never be shaken in a cocktail shaker. Rinse shaker out thoroughly after each use and dry with a clean lint-free cloth. This will ensure that your drinks only have in them what they are supposed to and will not distort the flavour of the next drink that you prepare.

Stirring – Where ingredients are required to be stirred, half fill a mixing glass

with ice and pour the ingredients over the ice. Stir and strain into chosen glass. Usually ingredients that mix easily together are prepared in this manner. Certain shooters require ingredients to be poured directly into chosen glass then stirred and served.

Building – To build a drink is to pour ingredients in order given into chosen glass over ice and serve with a swizzle stick or straw for the recipient to admire and stir.

Layering – To layer a drink is to pour ingredients in order given (pour over the back of a spoon into chosen glass). This will allow the liquid to flow down the inside rim of glass, creating a layering effect. Usually the heavier ingredients are poured first.

Useful Tips

Sugar syrup – To make sugar syrup bring one cup of ordinary white sugar with one cup of water almost to the boil in a small saucepan stirring continuously and simmer until sugar is completely dissolved. Then remove from heat and allow to cool. Once cool, pour into a re-sealable container or a corked bottle and store in refrigerator or behind your bar for regular use. This syrup will now last indefinitely.

Sweet and sour mix – To make sweet and sour mix bring one cup of sugar syrup to the simmer then add ½ cup fresh lemon juice and ½ cup fresh lime juice. Simmer till well mixed stirring frequently, then remove from heat and allow to cool. Once cool, pour into a re-sealable container or corked bottle and store in refrigerator for up to one to two weeks. Sweet and sour mix is also referred to as sour mix or bar mix.

To chill a glass – Glasses can be chilled by placing them into a refrigerator or by placing ice cubes into the glasses while drinks are being prepared. Discard these ice cubes before pouring unless otherwise instructed. It is more practical to refrigerate glasses for shooters due to the smaller size of glasses required for shooters.

To frost a glass – Where ingredients are required to be poured into a frosted glass, these glasses can be frosted by placing them into a freezer prior to use.

Fruit, peels and juices – Fruit slices and pieces will keep fresher and longer if covered with a damp clean linen cloth and refrigerated. When juices are required remember – fresh is best. When using canned fruit and/or juices, transfer the can's contents into appropriate re-sealable containers and refrigerate.

Ice – It is important to maintain a clean ice supply, as many shooters require ice during construction. To obtain crushed ice if you do not have access to an ice-crushing machine, place required ice onto a clean linen cloth and fold up. Place ice-filled cloth onto a hard surface and smash with a mallet – (not a bottle).

Glassware

Glasses come in a wide variety of shapes and sizes and range in value depending upon the quality of glass. When washing glasses, use hot water without detergent as detergent can distort the flavour of a drink or reduce the fizz in an effervescent drink. Only wash one glass at a time and dry with a clean lint-free cloth. Before using a glass, give it a quick polish with a glass cloth and check glass for chips and/or cracks. When handling glassware, hold glasses by their base or stem, as this will avoid finger marks around the rim of glass, thus maintaining a high polish.

The following is a compiled list of glassware required for shooters within this publication, although for the home bar an extensive range of glassware is not always necessary. As an example, a liqueur glass could be used as a cordial glass.

Cocktail	90ml (3fl oz) – 140ml ($4^2/_3$fl oz)
Collins	360ml (12fl oz)
Cordial	30ml (1fl oz) – 90ml (3fl oz)
Highball	300ml (10fl oz)
Liqueur	30ml (1fl oz) – 90ml (3fl oz)
Old-Fashioned	180ml (6fl oz) – 290ml ($9^2/_3$fl oz)
Pousse Café	90ml (3fl oz) – 120ml (4fl oz)
Shot	30ml (1fl oz) – 60ml (2fl oz)
Test Tube	Various Sizes

Bar Equipment

Before purchasing any bar equipment, have a search through your kitchen as the majority of households contain a selection of items required for your bar. The following is a list of the basic essential equipment required for your bar.

BAR EQUIPMENT

Blender	Corkscrew	Knives	Spoons
Bottle Opener	Cutting Board	Mixing Glass	Stirrers
Bottle Stoppers	Fruit Juicer	Napkins	Straws
Can Opener	Glass Cloth	Soda Siphon	Swizzle Sticks
Coasters	Hawthorn	Spirit Measures	Toothpicks
Cocktail Shaker	Strainer	Sponge	
	Ice Bucket and		
	Tongs		

Your Own Bar

Before you make a purchase of a bar, it is advisable to visit pubs, clubs, cocktail bars or friends that may have home bars. By doing this, it will assist in providing you with a broader spectrum on what sort of bar would best suit you. This will also provide you with ideas on lighting, what they have in common and what appeals to you personally. Also take into consideration how much room you have for a bar and your budget.

Measures

1 Dash	1ml (1/30fl oz)
1 Teaspoon	5ml (1/6fl oz)
1 Cup	250ml (8$\frac{1}{3}$fl oz)

There are many different sizes and styles of bars. The three main categories are:

Mobile Bar – The purpose of a mobile bar is that it can be moved easily to a position from which you wish to serve, e.g., room to room or indoors to outdoors.

Semi-Permanent Bar – This is a bar that is a main feature of a room to be intended as a showpiece where glassware and bottles can be displayed. This style of bar should be erected as close to washing up facilities as is practical.

Permanent Bar – A permanent bar can turn a room into a bar room containing a built-in sink behind the bar with hot and cold water, a fridge/freezer, equipment and accessories. Glass shelving with mirrored backing provides the opportunity to place your glassware and bottles on display. Mood lighting can be used to great effect in such a room. Adding a couple of matching bar stools and a couple of lounges makes for the perfect room to retire to after that long day's work, not to mention cocktail parties that you could hold in style.

SPIRITS	LIQUEURS
Bacardi	Advocaat
Bourbon	Amaretto
Brandy	Bailey's Irish Cream
Cognac	Banana Liqueur
Dark Rum	Chambord
Gin	Cointreau
Light Rum	Crème De Cacao
Malibu	Crème De Menthe
Schnapps	Curaçao
Scotch Whisky	Drambuie
Southern Comfort	Galliano
Tequila	Grand Marnier
Vodka	Jägermeister
	Kahlúa
	Midori
	Sambuca
	Strawberry Liqueur
	Tia Maria

COMMON MIXERS AND ADDITIVES

Apple Juice	Cranberry Juice
Grapefruit Juice	Lemon Juice
Lime Juice	Milk
Pineapple Juice	Sweet and Sour Mix
Cola	Cream
Lemonade	Lemon-Lime Soda
Mango Juice	Orange Juice
Soda Water	Tabasco Sauce

Hosting a Party

To be the host of a party can be stressful if you are not properly prepared. Here are some helpful hints to ensure that you and your guests enjoy the occasion.

It is advisable to pre-cut your fruit for garnishes and wrap them in plastic or place a clean damp linen cloth over them and refrigerate until required. Juices should be squeezed and/or removed from tin cans. Pour juices into re-sealable containers and refrigerate. Make up a bowl of sugar syrup as described under useful tips. This will save you from having to dissolve sugar when preparing large quantities of drinks. Keep a glass of water on your bar for rinsing instruments such as spoons and stirrers. If your washing machine is in close proximity to your bar or kitchen, it can be used to fill with clean fresh ice. This will keep the ice chilled and will be less mess to clean up during and after your party. As well as having a good supply of alcohol, you should also be sure to have a fair selection of non-alcoholic drinks for those guests who choose not to participate in the consumption of alcohol.

If you find yourself hosting a large party, it is an idea to make yourself a checklist of what you require and what must be completed. Once your list is all checked off, you should then be able to sit down and relax before your home is invaded by guests. Then you can enjoy delectable cocktails with family and friends without the stress of hosting the occasion.

Cordials and Liqueurs

Cordials and liqueurs are alcohol-based with herbs, aromatic plants, essences, juices, beans, nuts, dairy products, sweeteners and colours which are infused in the spirit by the process of steeping and distillation.

Cordials and liqueurs date back centuries. In 1510 Bénédictine DOM was created by a Benedictine monk making it one of the world's oldest known liqueurs. The recipe for Bénédictine still remains a closely guarded secret as is the case for many cordials and liqueurs.

Traditionally, cordials and liqueurs were created for medicinal purposes as a cure for all types of ills. Creating cordials and liqueurs hundreds of years ago meant that people would gather herbs, fruits and plants from their gardens and then added them with sugar to liquors such as Gin, Brandy and other

liquors. Today cordials and liqueurs are produced by distilling companies worldwide. It would not be possible to list all cordials and liqueurs that are being produced or available. A list has been provided of the main ones that are required for shooters in the introduction of this book.

Cordials and liqueurs are essential ingredients in a vast variety of shooters.

Shooters

Shooters originated in America where liquors such as Scotch Whisky or Bourbon were served in shot glasses, with other liqueurs added to metamorphosis.

The ingredients of each drink are required to be layered in order given to create a layered effect. Pour ingredients slowly over the back of a spoon that touches the inside of glass, allowing the liquid to flow slowly down the inside of glass. The heavier ingredients are usually poured first to create the greatest visual effect. The ingredients for some shooters are shaken or stirred over ice and then poured into selected glass to be served as a shooter or shot.

Shooters can be served in shot glasses, cocktail glasses, liqueur glasses, cordial glasses or test tubes and should be swallowed in one gulp. Other glasses such as old-fashioned glasses are required for certain shooters.

KAHLÚA

BACKFIRE

24.7% alc/vol
0.6 standard drinks

10ml (¹/₃fl oz) Kahlúa
10ml (¹/₃fl oz) Bailey's Irish Cream
10ml (¹/₃fl oz) Vodka

Layer ingredients in order given into a cordial embassy glass and serve.

RHINO

25.7% alc/vol
0.9 standard drinks

15ml (½fl oz) Kahlúa
15ml (½fl oz) Cointreau
15ml (½fl oz) Amarula Cream

Layer ingredients in order given into a tall dutch cordial glass and serve.

Backfire

CHOCOLATE SUNDAE

15.1% alc/vol
0.5 standard drinks

10ml (¹/₃fl oz) Kahlúa
10ml (¹/₃fl oz) Bailey's Irish Cream
10ml (¹/₃fl oz) White Crème De Cacao
Fresh Whipped Cream (chilled)

Layer ingredients in order given into a cordial lexington glass, float cream on top and serve.

INNOCENT EYES

25.1% alc/vol
0.6 standard drinks

10ml (¹/₃fl oz) Kahlúa
10ml (¹/₃fl oz) Sambuca
10ml (¹/₃fl oz) Bailey's Irish Cream

Layer ingredients in order given into a cordial embassy glass and serve.

Chocolate Sundae

LAVA LAMP

21.1% alc/vol
0.5 standard drinks

8ml (¼fl oz) Kahlúa
8ml (¼fl oz) Strawberry Liqueur
8ml (¼fl oz) Frangelico
8ml (¼fl oz) Bailey's Irish Cream
3 drops Advocaat

Pour kahlúa, liqueur and frangelico into a shot glass – do not stir.
Layer bailey's on top and add advocaat by drops then serve.

PEPPERMINT PATTIE

13.3% alc/vol
0.5 standard drinks

15ml (½fl oz) Kahlúa
15ml (½fl oz) Peppermint Schnapps
15ml (½fl oz) Fresh Cream (chilled)

Pour ingredients into a cocktail shaker over ice and shake. Strain into
a chilled shot glass and serve.

Lava Lamp

1 MIND ERASER

7.1% alc/vol
1.3 standard drinks

30ml (1fl oz) Kahlúa
30ml (1fl oz) Vodka
180ml (6fl oz) Soda Water

Build ingredients in order given into a collins glass over ice and serve with a straw. Insert straw to bottom of drink whilst having finger placed over top of straw then drink through straw quickly as a shot.

MÉNAGE À TROIS SHOOTER

28% alc/vol
0.7 standard drinks

10ml (1/3fl oz) Kahlúa
10ml (1/3fl oz) Grand Marnier
10ml (1/3fl oz) Frangelico

Layer ingredients in order given into a cordial embassy glass and serve.

APACHE

19.4% alc/vol
1.4 standard drinks

30ml (1fl oz) Kahlúa
30ml (1fl oz) Bailey's Irish Cream
30ml (1fl oz) Midori

Layer ingredients in order given into a pousse café glass and serve.

FLYING MONKEY

20.1% alc/vol
0.5 standard drinks

10ml (1/3fl oz) Kahlúa
10ml (1/3fl oz) Bailey's Irish Cream
10ml (1/3fl oz) Banana Liqueur

Layer ingredients in order given into a cordial embassy glass and serve.

25

NAPALM-DEATH

29.3% alc/vol
0.9 standard drinks

10ml (1/3fl oz) Kahlúa
10ml (1/3fl oz) Drambuie
10ml (1/3fl oz) Bailey's Irish Cream
10ml (1/3fl oz) Cointreau

Layer ingredients in order given into a tall dutch cordial glass and serve.

BIRTH MARK

22.6% alc/vol
0.4 standard drinks

5ml (1/6fl oz) Kahlúa
5ml (1/6fl oz) White Crème De Cacao
10ml (1/3fl oz) Tia Maria
5ml (1/6fl oz) Bailey's Irish Cream

Layer ingredients in order given into a cordial embassy glass and serve.
This shooter was created by the author of this book.

Birth Mark

RAIJA

10% alc/vol
0.3 standard drinks

8ml (¼fl oz) Kahlúa
8ml (¼fl oz) Vanilla Liqueur
8ml (¼fl oz) Mango Juice
8ml (¼fl oz) Fresh Orange Juice

Pour ingredients into a cocktail shaker over ice and shake. Strain into a chilled shot glass and serve.

B-52

21.7% alc/vol
0.5 standard drinks

10ml ($^1/_3$fl oz) Kahlúa
10ml ($^1/_3$fl oz) Bailey's Irish Cream
10ml ($^1/_3$fl oz) Amaretto

Layer ingredients in order given into a test tube and serve.

Q.F.

19.7% alc/vol
0.5 standard drinks

12ml (²/₅fl oz) Kahlúa
12ml (²/₅fl oz) Midori
8ml (¼fl oz) Bailey's Irish Cream

Layer ingredients in order given into a cordial embassy glass and serve.

VODKA

APPLE PIE SHOT

28.1% alc/vol
1 standard drink

30ml (1fl oz) Vodka
5ml (1/6fl oz) Cinnamon Schnapps
8ml (¼fl oz) Apple Juice

Pour ingredients into a mixing glass over ice and stir. Strain into a chilled shot glass and serve.

CHRISTMAS TREE

27.6% alc/vol
1 standard drink

15ml (½fl oz) Vodka
15ml (½fl oz) Green Crème De Menthe
15ml (½fl oz) Cherry Brandy

Layer ingredients in order given into a tall dutch cordial glass and serve.

Christmas Tree

SWEDISH COLOR

28.3% alc/vol
0.7 standard drinks

10ml (¹/₃fl oz) Vodka
10ml (¹/₃fl oz) Banana Liqueur
10ml (¹/₃fl oz) Blue Curaçao

Layer ingredients in order given into a cordial embassy glass and serve.

SPOT SHOOTER

27.9% alc/vol
1 standard drink

23ml (¾fl oz) Vodka
23ml (¾fl oz) Kahlúa
4 drops Bailey's Irish Cream

Pour vodka into a tall dutch cordial glass and layer kahlúa on top.
Add bailey's by drops and serve.

Swedish Color

ESTONIAN FOREST FIRE

34.7% alc/vol
0.9 standard drinks

30ml (1fl oz) Vodka
12 drops Tabasco Sauce
1 Fresh Kiwi Fruit

Pour vodka and sauce into a shot glass. Stir and serve with a kiwi fruit – to be consumed after shooting.

BOLCHEVICH

14.3% alc/vol
0.5 standard drinks

10ml (^{1}/₃fl oz) Vodka (chilled)
10ml (^{1}/₃fl oz) Fresh Milk (chilled)
10ml (^{1}/₃fl oz) Sweet and Sour Mix (chilled)
10ml (^{1}/₃fl oz) Raspberry Liqueur (chilled)

Layer ingredients in order given into a frosted shot glass and serve.

Estonian Forest Fire

STAINED BLUE DRESS

31% alc/vol
0.7 standard drinks

15ml (½fl oz) Vodka
15ml (½fl oz) Blue Curaçao
2 drops Bailey's Irish Cream

Pour vodka into a cordial embassy glass and layer curaçao on top.
Add bailey's by drops and serve.

ICY AFTER EIGHT

22.5% alc/vol
0.8 standard drinks

23ml (¾fl oz) Vodka
8ml (¼fl oz) Green Crème De Menthe
15ml (½fl oz) Chocolate Syrup

Pour ingredients into a cocktail shaker over a crushed ice cube and shake
well. Pour into a chilled shot glass and serve.

Stained Blue Dress

RUSSIAN CANDY

27.6% alc/vol
0.7 standard drinks

15ml (½fl oz) Vodka
15ml (½fl oz) Peach Schnapps
Dash Grenadine

Pour vodka and schnapps into a shot glass then stir. Add grenadine and allow to settle on bottom of drink then serve.

ASTRONAUT SHOOTER

34.2% alc/vol
1.8 standard drinks

60ml (2fl oz) Vodka
Wedge of Lemon
Pinch of Coffee Powder
Pinch of Sugar

Sprinkle coffee powder over one side of lemon wedge and sugar over other side. Pour vodka into a mixing glass over ice and stir to chill then strain into a chilled large shot glass. Suck the lemon then shoot the vodka.

SPECIAL EMOTION

24.4% alc/vol
0.5 standard drinks

5ml (¹⁄₆fl oz) Vodka
5ml (¹⁄₆fl oz) Fresh Orange Juice
5ml (¹⁄₆fl oz) Dark Rum
5ml (¹⁄₆fl oz) Triple Sec
5ml (¹⁄₆fl oz) Parfait Amour

Layer ingredients in order given into a cordial embassy glass and serve.

THE END OF THE WORLD

54.2% alc/vol
1.9 standard drinks

15ml (½fl oz) Vodka
15ml (½fl oz) 151-Proof Bacardi
15ml (½fl oz) 101-Proof Wild Turkey Bourbon

Pour ingredients in order given into a shot glass – do not stir, then serve.

SUITABLY FRANK

30.3% alc/vol
1.1 standard drinks

15ml (½fl oz) Vodka
15ml (½fl oz) Licor 43
15ml (½fl oz) Cherry Brandy

Layer ingredients in order given into a tall dutch cordial glass and serve.

69ER IN A POOL

54.4% alc/vol
1.3 standard drinks

15ml (½fl oz) Vodka
Dash Fresh Lemon Juice
15ml (½fl oz) 151-Proof Bacardi
Drop of Tabasco Sauce

Layer ingredients in order given into a shot glass and serve.

JAMBOREE

24.5% alc/vol
0.7 standard drinks

15ml (½fl oz) Vodka
15ml (½fl oz) Wilderberry Schnapps
5ml (1/6fl oz) Cranberry Juice

Pour ingredients into a mixing glass over ice and stir. Strain into a chilled shot glass and serve.

BAILEY'S IRISH CREAM

ECHO HAEMORRHAGING TUMOR

17.3% alc/vol
0.4 standard drinks

30ml (1fl oz) Bailey's Irish Cream
6 drops Blue Curaçao
8 drops Strawberry Schnapps

Pour bailey's into a shot glass and add curaçao by drops. Add schnapps by drops and serve.

EASY DOES IT

44% alc/vol
1.6 standard drinks

15ml (½fl oz) Bailey's Irish Cream
15ml (½fl oz) Kahlúa
15ml (½fl oz) Everclear

Pour bailey's into a shot glass and add kahlúa – do not stir. Layer everclear on top and serve.

Echo Haemorrhaging Tumor

AFTERBIRTH

12.4% alc/vol
0.4 standard drinks

15ml (½fl oz) Bailey's Irish Cream
15ml (½fl oz) Raspberry Schnapps
15ml (½fl oz) Grenadine

Pour schnapps and grenadine into a shot glass then stir. Layer bailey's on top and serve.

BLACK FOREST CAKE

20.1% alc/vol
0.7 standard drinks

15ml (½fl oz) Bailey's Irish Cream
15ml (½fl oz) Cherry Brandy
15ml (½fl oz) Kahlúa

Pour brandy and kahlúa into a cocktail shaker over ice. Shake and strain into a chilled tall dutch cordial glass. Layer bailey's on top and serve.

Afterbirth

WET PUSSY

7.6% alc/vol
0.3 standard drinks

15ml (½fl oz) Bailey's Irish Cream
10ml (1/3fl oz) Chambord
30ml (1fl oz) Milk (chilled)

Pour ingredients into a cocktail shaker over ice and shake. Strain into
a chilled tall dutch cordial glass and serve.

CONCRETE

27% alc/vol
0.3 standard drinks

30ml (1fl oz) Bailey's Irish Cream
30ml (1fl oz) Vodka

Pour bailey's into a shot glass and pour vodka into a separate shot glass.
To consume: first pour vodka into mouth and then bailey's into mouth.
Swish around and swallow.

Wet Pussy

BRAIN SHOOTER

24.7% alc/vol
0.6 standard drinks

23ml (¾fl oz) Bailey's Irish Cream
8ml (¼fl oz) Rumplemintz
Dash Grenadine

Pour bailey's and rumplemintz into a shot glass then stir. Add grenadine
by drops into centre of drink – do not stir, then serve.

JUICY PUSSY

12.4% alc/vol
0.4 standard drinks

15ml (½fl oz) Bailey's Irish Cream
15ml (½fl oz) Peach Schnapps
15ml (½fl oz) Pineapple Juice

Pour ingredients into a cocktail shaker over ice and shake. Strain into
a chilled shot glass and serve.

KILTED BLACK LEPRECHAUN

26% alc/vol
0.6 standard drinks

10ml (¹/₃fl oz) Bailey's Irish Cream
10ml (¹/₃fl oz) Malibu
10ml (¹/₃fl oz) Drambuie

Pour ingredients gently in order given into a cordial embassy glass – do not
stir, then serve.

JOHN DOE

20.7% alc/vol
0.7 standard drinks

15ml (½fl oz) Bailey's Irish Cream
15ml (½fl oz) Raspberry Liqueur
15ml (½fl oz) Triple Sec

Pour ingredients into a cocktail shaker over ice and shake. Strain into
a chilled shot glass and serve.

I.R.A.

32.4% alc/vol
0.8 standard drinks

10ml (1/3fl oz) Bailey's Irish Cream
10ml (1/3fl oz) Irish Mist
10ml (1/3fl oz) Irish Whiskey

Pour ingredients into a shot glass, stir and serve.

ELECTRICAL STORM

29% alc/vol
0.7 standard drinks

8ml (¼fl oz) Bailey's Irish Cream
8ml (¼fl oz) Peppermint Schnapps
8ml (¼fl oz) Goldschläger
8ml (¼fl oz) Jägermeister

Layer ingredients in order given into a cordial embassy glass and serve.

AMARETTO

CHOCOLATE ALMOND

22.7% alc/vol
0.5 standard drinks

10ml (¹/₃fl oz) Amaretto
10ml (¹/₃fl oz) Bailey's Irish Cream
10ml (¹/₃fl oz) Dark Crème De Cacao

Layer ingredients in order given into a cordial embassy glass and serve.

PLACENTA

21.8% alc/vol
0.5 standard drinks

15ml (½fl oz) Amaretto
15ml (½fl oz) Bailey's Irish Cream
3 drops Grenadine

Pour amaretto into a cordial embassy glass and add bailey's – do not stir.
Add grenadine by drops and serve.

Placenta

GOLDEN FLASH

30.3% alc/vol
0.7 standard drinks

10ml (¹/₃fl oz) Amaretto
10ml (¹/₃fl oz) Triple Sec
10ml (¹/₃fl oz) Sambuca

Layer ingredients in order given into a cordial embassy glass and serve.

ROMONA BANANA

23.7% alc/vol
0.6 standard drinks

10ml (¹/₃fl oz) Amaretto
10ml (¹/₃fl oz) Peppermint Schnapps
10ml (¹/₃fl oz) Banana Liqueur

Layer ingredients in order given into a cordial embassy glass and serve.

Golden Flash

STORMCLOUD

32.2% alc/vol
0.9 standard drinks

23ml (¾fl oz) Amaretto
8ml (¼fl oz) Bailey's Irish Cream
5ml ($1/6$fl oz) 151-Proof Bacardi

Layer ingredients in order given into a cordial embassy glass and serve.

WET KISS

16% alc/vol
0.6 standard drinks

15ml (½fl oz) Amaretto
15ml (½fl oz) Watermelon Schnapps
15ml (½fl oz) Sweet and Sour Mix

Layer ingredients in order given into a tall dutch cordial glass and serve.

Stormcloud

DOUCET DEVIL

29% alc/vol
0.7 standard drinks

15ml (½fl oz) Amaretto
8ml (¼fl oz) Southern Comfort
8ml (¼fl oz) Banana Liqueur

Layer ingredients in order given into a cordial embassy glass and serve.

MUD SLIDE

24.8% alc/vol
0.9 standard drinks

15ml (½fl oz) Amaretto
15ml (½fl oz) Peppermint Schnapps
15ml (½fl oz) Tia Maria

Pour ingredients into a cocktail shaker over ice and shake. Strain into
a chilled shot glass and serve.

LITTLE BITCH

24.4% alc/vol
0.8 standard drinks

15ml (½fl oz) Amaretto
15ml (½fl oz) Southern Comfort
5ml (¹/₆fl oz) Cranberry Juice
5ml (¹/₆fl oz) Fresh Orange Juice

Pour ingredients into a cocktail shaker over ice and shake. Strain into a chilled shot glass and serve.

B-28

19.9% alc/vol
0.9 standard drinks

10ml (¹/₃fl oz) Amaretto
10ml (¹/₃fl oz) Kahlúa
30ml (1fl oz) Bailey's Irish Cream
10ml (¹/₃fl oz) Butterscotch Schnapps

Layer ingredients in order given into a liqueur glass and serve.

JELLYFISH

23.2% alc/vol
0.7 standard drinks

15ml (½fl oz) Amaretto
15ml (½fl oz) Dark Crème De Cacao
8ml (¼fl oz) Bailey's Irish Cream
3 drops Grenadine

Pour amaretto and cacao into a shot glass – do not stir. Layer bailey's on top and add grenadine by drops then serve.

BRAIN DESTROYER

23.4% alc/vol
0.6 standard drinks

10ml (^{1}/$_3$fl oz) Amaretto
10ml (^{1}/$_3$fl oz) Bailey's Irish Cream
10ml (^{1}/$_3$fl oz) Kahlúa
Dash 151-Proof Bacardi

Pour amaretto, bailey's and kahlúa into a shot glass then stir briefly. Add bacardi – do not stir, then serve.

Jellyfish

RED LOBSTER

27.9% alc/vol
0.8 standard drinks

15ml (½fl oz) Amaretto
15ml (½fl oz) Southern Comfort
5ml (1/6fl oz) Cranberry Juice

Pour ingredients into a cocktail shaker over ice and shake. Strain into a chilled shot glass and serve.

Rum

TROPICAL PASSION

25.5% alc/vol
0.9 standard drinks

10ml ($^1/_3$fl oz) Light Rum
10ml ($^1/_3$fl oz) Peach Schnapps
10ml ($^1/_3$fl oz) Sloe Gin
10ml ($^1/_3$fl oz) Triple Sec
3 dashes Fresh Orange Juice

Pour ingredients into a cocktail shaker over ice and shake. Strain into a chilled shot glass and serve.

DEATH ROW

57.8% alc/vol
1.4 standard drinks

15ml (½fl oz) 151-Proof Bacardi
15ml (½fl oz) Tennessee Whiskey

Pour ingredients into a shot glass, stir and serve.

Tropical Passion

BIG PINE PUSS

23.3% alc/vol
0.4 standard drinks

30ml (1fl oz) Spiced Rum
15ml (½fl oz) Banana Liqueur
5ml (1/6fl oz) Grenadine
5ml (1/6fl oz) Cranberry Juice
5ml (1/6fl oz) Fresh Lime Juice

Pour ingredients into a mixing glass over ice and stir. Strain into a chilled old-fashioned glass and serve as a shooter.

NYMPHOMANIAC

27.8% alc/vol
1.3 standard drinks

30ml (1fl oz) Spiced Rum
15ml (½fl oz) Malibu
15ml (½fl oz) Peach Schnapps

Pour ingredients into a cocktail shaker over ice and shake. Strain into a chilled large shot glass and serve.

Big Pine Puss

BUONASERA SHOOTER

30.4% alc/vol
1.1 standard drinks

15ml (½fl oz) Vanilla Rum
15ml (½fl oz) Tia Maria
15ml (½fl oz) Amaretto

Layer ingredients in order given into a tall dutch cordial glass and serve.

THE ANTICHRIST

62.9% alc/vol
1.6 standard drinks

10ml ($^1/_3$fl oz) 151-Proof Bacardi
10ml ($^1/_3$fl oz) Everclear
10ml ($^1/_3$fl oz) Pepper Vodka
3 dashes Tabasco Sauce

Pour ingredients in order given into a shot glass – do not stir, then serve.

The Antichrist

VULCAN MIND PROBE

37.5% alc/vol
1.2 standard drinks

20ml (²/₃fl oz) Light Rum
20ml (²/₃fl oz) Ouzo

Pour ingredients into a shot glass, stir and serve.

BACKDRAFT

29% alc/vol
1.4 standard drinks

30ml (1fl oz) Light Rum
30ml (1fl oz) Cinnamon Schnapps

Pour ingredients in order given into a large shot glass – do not stir, then serve.

THREE STAGES OF FRIENDSHIP

51.1% alc/vol
1.2 standard drinks

10ml (¹/₃fl oz) 151-Proof Rum
10ml (¹/₃fl oz) Tennessee Whiskey
10ml (¹/₃fl oz) Tequila

Pour ingredients into a shot glass, stir and serve.

HORSEMEN OF THE APOCALYPSE

38.3% alc/vol
1.2 standard drinks

10ml (¹/₃fl oz) Spiced Rum
10ml (¹/₃fl oz) Tennessee Whiskey
10ml (¹/₃fl oz) Tequila
10ml (¹/₃fl oz) Bourbon

Pour each ingredient into individual shot glasses and shoot one after the other in order given.

SWEET SHOT

31% alc/vol
0.8 standard drinks

15ml (½fl oz) Dark Rum
8ml (¼fl oz) Coconut Liqueur
8ml (¼fl oz) Amaretto

Layer ingredients in order given into a cordial lexington glass and serve.

TWIN SISTERS

34% alc/vol
0.9 standard drinks

15ml (½fl oz) Bacardi
15ml (½fl oz) Spiced Rum
Dash Rose's Lime Juice
Dash Cola

Pour bacardi, rum and juice into a cocktail shaker over ice. Shake and strain into a chilled shot glass. Add cola – do not stir, then serve.

Sweet Shot

CARIBBEAN SWIM

20% alc/vol
1.1 standard drinks

23ml (¾fl oz) Spiced Rum
15ml (½fl oz) Brandy
30ml (1fl oz) Cranberry Juice

Pour ingredients into a cocktail shaker over ice and shake. Strain into two chilled shot glasses and serve.

SCHNAPPS

DAMN GOOD!

15.9% alc/vol
0.5 standard drinks

15ml (½fl oz) Butterscotch Schnapps
8ml (¼fl oz) Green Crème De Menthe
8ml (¼fl oz) Bailey's Irish Cream
8ml (¼fl oz) Grenadine

Pour schnapps into a cordial lexington glass and layer crème de menthe on top. Layer bailey's on top and slowly add grenadine by pouring down inside rim of glass, allow to settle on bottom of drink then serve.

BARMAN'S BREAKFAST

19.3% alc/vol
0.7 standard drinks

30ml (1fl oz) Peach Schnapps
15ml (½fl oz) Advocaat

Layer ingredients in order given into a shot glass and serve.

Damn Good!

ILLICIT AFFAIR

13.9% alc/vol
0.4 standard drinks

15ml (½fl oz) Peppermint Schnapps
15ml (½fl oz) Bailey's Irish Cream
Fresh Whipped Cream (chilled)

Layer ingredients in order given into a tall dutch cordial glass, float cream on top and serve.

SEX IN THE PARKING LOT

24.5% alc/vol
0.9 standard drinks

15ml (½fl oz) Apple Schnapps
15ml (½fl oz) Chambord
15ml (½fl oz) Vodka

Pour ingredients into a cocktail shaker over ice and shake. Strain into a chilled shot glass and serve.

JAM DOUGHNUT

18.4% alc/vol
0.5 standard drinks

20ml (²/₃fl oz) Butterscotch Schnapps
10ml (¹/₃fl oz) Bailey's Irish Cream
Dash Grenadine

Layer ingredients in order given into a cordial embassy glass and serve.

DEATH BY FIRE

13.3% alc/vol
0.3 standard drinks

10ml (¹/₃fl oz) Cinnamon Schnapps
10ml (¹/₃fl oz) Peppermint Schnapps
10ml (¹/₃fl oz) Tabasco Sauce

Pour ingredients into a shot glass, stir and serve.

BRAIN HAEMORRHAGE

18% alc/vol
0.5 standard drinks

30ml (1fl oz) Peach Schnapps
5ml (¹⁄₆fl oz) Bailey's Irish Cream
3 dashes Grenadine

Pour schnapps into a test tube then add bailey's and allow to settle on bottom of drink. Add grenadine – do not stir, then serve.

VANILLA KISS

6.7% alc/vol
0.2 standard drinks

15ml (½fl oz) Vanilla Schnapps
15ml (½fl oz) Hot Cocoa
15ml (½fl oz) Fresh Cream (chilled)

Layer ingredients in order given into a tall dutch cordial glass and serve.

Brain Haemorrhage

PIERCED BUTTERY NIPPLE

24.1% alc/vol
0.9 standard drinks

15ml (½fl oz) Butterscotch Schnapps
15ml (½fl oz) Bailey's Irish Cream
15ml (½fl oz) Jägermeister

Layer ingredients in order given into a tall dutch cordial glass and serve.

MINT SLICE

20% alc/vol
0.7 standard drinks

30ml (1fl oz) Peppermint Schnapps
15ml (½fl oz) Kahlúa

Layer ingredients in order given into a shot glass and serve.

Mint Slice

LEATHER WHIP

30.8% alc/vol
0.8 standard drinks

8ml (¼fl oz) Peach Schnapps
8ml (¼fl oz) Tennessee Whiskey
8ml (¼fl oz) Tequila
8ml (¼fl oz) Triple Sec

Pour ingredients into a shot glass, stir and serve.

PINK PANTY

27.6% alc/vol
0.7 standard drinks

15ml (½fl oz) Cinnamon Schnapps
15ml (½fl oz) Vodka
Dash Cranberry Juice

Pour schnapps and vodka into a cocktail shaker over ice. Shake and strain into a chilled shot glass. Add juice – do not stir, then serve.

FLIRTING CARRIES

22.7% alc/vol
0.8 standard drinks

15ml (½fl oz) Peach Schnapps
15ml (½fl oz) Strawberry Liqueur
15ml (½fl oz) Triple Sec

Layer ingredients in order given into a tall dutch cordial glass and serve.

COCK SUCKING COWBOY

19.5% alc/vol
0.5 standard drinks

30ml (1fl oz) Butterscotch Schnapps
5ml (1/6fl oz) Bailey's Irish Cream

Layer ingredients in order given into a shot glass and serve.

DOOR COUNTY CHERRY CHEESECAKE

9.5% alc/vol
0.7 standard drinks

45ml (1½fl oz) Vanilla Schnapps
30ml (1fl oz) Maraschino Cherry Juice
15ml (½fl oz) Cranberry Juice
5ml (1/6fl oz) Fresh Cream (chilled)

Pour ingredients into a cocktail shaker over ice and shake. Strain into three chilled shot glasses and serve.

FLAMING

BOB MARLEY SHOT

42.4% alc/vol
1 standard drink

15ml (½fl oz) 151-Proof Bacardi
8ml (¼fl oz) White Crème De Menthe
8ml (¼fl oz) Grenadine

Pour grenadine and crème de menthe into a shot glass – do not stir. Layer bacardi on top and ignite then serve with a straw.

FLAMING BLUE

26% alc/vol
0.7 standard drinks

15ml (½fl oz) Anisette
15ml (½fl oz) Dry Vermouth
5ml (¹⁄₆fl oz) Bacardi

Pour anisette and vermouth into a shot glass. Stir and layer bacardi on top. Ignite then extinguish flame and serve.

Bob Marley Shot

FLAMING ARMADILLO

37.7% alc/vol
1.3 standard drinks

20ml (²/₃fl oz) Tequila
20ml (²/₃fl oz) Amaretto
5ml (¹/₆fl oz) 151-Proof Rum

Layer ingredients in order given into a shot glass, ignite and shoot while flaming.

ARRACK ATTACK

34.8% alc/vol
1.4 standard drinks

20ml (²/₃fl oz) Green Crème De Menthe
20ml (²/₃fl oz) Arrack
10ml (¹/₃fl oz) Sambuca

Layer ingredients in order given into a liqueur glass, ignite and serve with a straw.

FLAMING COURAGE

33.9% alc/vol
0.9 standard drinks

10ml ($^1/_3$fl oz) Midori
10ml ($^1/_3$fl oz) Peppermint Schnapps
10ml ($^1/_3$fl oz) Aftershock
5ml ($^1/_6$fl oz) 151-Proof Bacardi

Layer ingredients in order given into a shot glass, ignite and shoot
while flaming.

INFERNO

63.9% alc/vol
1.6 standard drinks

15ml (½fl oz) Everclear
15ml (½fl oz) Pepper Vodka
6 drops Tabasco Sauce
Pinch of Salt

Pour sauce into a shot glass then add vodka and everclear – do not stir.
Sprinkle salt on top, ignite and serve.

FIERY BLUE MUSTANG

47.6% alc/vol
1.7 standard drinks

15ml (½fl oz) Banana Liqueur
15ml (½fl oz) Blue Curaçao
15ml (½fl oz) Everclear

Pour ingredients into a shot glass and stir. Ignite then extinguish flame
and serve.

GREEN LIZARD

59.3% alc/vol
1.8 standard drinks

30ml (1fl oz) Green Chartreuse
8ml (¼fl oz) 151-Proof Bacardi

Layer ingredients in order given into a shot glass, ignite and serve.

Fiery Blue Mustang

CONCORD

35.2% alc/vol
1.1 standard drinks

15ml (½fl oz) Tia Maria
15ml (½fl oz) Bailey's Irish Cream
10ml (⅓fl oz) 151-Proof Bacardi

Layer ingredients in order given into a shot glass, ignite and serve.

FLAMING GORILLA

38.4% alc/vol
1.4 standard drinks

15ml (½fl oz) Peppermint Schnapps
15ml (½fl oz) Kahlúa
15ml (½fl oz) 151-Proof Bacardi

Layer ingredients in order given into a shot glass and ignite. Extinguish flame and serve.

Flaming Gorilla

FERRARI SHOOTER

32.3% alc/vol
1 standard drink

20ml (²/₃fl oz) Tia Maria
20ml (²/₃fl oz) Sambuca

Layer ingredients in order given into a shot glass, ignite and serve.

FLAMING RUSSIAN

49.8% alc/vol
1.8 standard drinks

30ml (1fl oz) Vodka
15ml (½fl oz) 151 Proof Bacardi

Layer ingredients in order given into a shot glass, ignite and serve.

Ferrari Shooter

LIBERACE

31.8% alc/vol
0.8 standard drinks

10ml (¹/₃fl oz) Kahlúa
10ml (¹/₃fl oz) Fresh Milk (chilled)
10ml (¹/₃fl oz) 151-Proof Bacardi

Layer ingredients in order given into a cordial embassy glass and ignite.
Extinguish flame and serve.

BANANA LIQUEUR
& MIDORI

SPERM SHOT

11.5% alc/vol
0.3 standard drinks

15ml (½fl oz) Banana Liqueur
15ml (½fl oz) Fresh Cream (chilled)

Pour ingredients into a shot glass, stir and serve.

MIDORI ILLUSION SHAKER

13.4% alc/vol
1.9 standard drinks

60ml (2fl oz) Midori
15ml (½fl oz) Cointreau
15ml (½fl oz) Vodka
60ml (2fl oz) Pineapple Juice
30ml (1fl oz) Fresh Lemon Juice

Pour ingredients into a cocktail shaker over ice and shake. Strain into four
chilled cocktail glasses and serve.

Midori Illusion Shaker

DOUBLE DATE

28% alc/vol
1 standard drink

15ml (½fl oz) Midori
15ml (½fl oz) White Crème De Menthe
15ml (½fl oz) Bénédictine

Layer ingredients in order given into a tall dutch cordial glass and serve.

BANSHEE BERRY

22% alc/vol
0.6 standard drinks

12ml (²/₅fl oz) Banana Liqueur
12ml (²/₅fl oz) Strawberry Schnapps
12ml (²/₅fl oz) White Crème De Cacao

Pour ingredients into a shot glass, stir and serve.

GREEN JOLLY RANCHER

24.9% alc/vol
0.7 standard drinks

15ml (½fl oz) Midori
15ml (½fl oz) Southern Comfort
5ml (¹⁄₆fl oz) Sweet and Sour Mix

Pour ingredients into a cocktail shaker over ice and shake. Strain into
a chilled shot glass and serve.

BLASTER

27.7% alc/vol
0.7 standard drinks

10ml (¹/₃fl oz) Banana Liqueur
10ml (¹/₃fl oz) Cointreau
10ml (¹/₃fl oz) Kahlúa

Layer ingredients in order given into a cordial embassy glass and serve.

GUMBALL HUMMER

14.4% alc/vol
0.5 standard drinks

15ml (½fl oz) Banana Liqueur
15ml (½fl oz) Raspberry Schnapps
15ml (½fl oz) Grapefruit Juice

Pour ingredients into a cocktail shaker over ice and shake. Strain into
a chilled shot glass and serve.

Blaster

HARD ROCKA

25% alc/vol
0.6 standard drinks

10ml (⅓fl oz) Midori
10ml (⅓fl oz) Vodka
10ml (⅓fl oz) Bailey's Irish Cream

Layer ingredients in order given into a cordial lexington glass and serve.

DEAD FROG

17.7% alc/vol
0.5 standard drinks

23ml (¾fl oz) Midori
8ml (¼fl oz) Bailey's Irish Cream
4 dashes Grenadine

Pour ingredients into a mixing glass over ice and stir. Strain into a chilled shot glass and serve.

Hard Rocka

E.T.

25% alc/vol
0.6 standard drinks

10ml (¹/₃fl oz) Midori
10ml (¹/₃fl oz) Bailey's Irish Cream
10ml (¹/₃fl oz) Vodka

Layer ingredients in order given into a shot glass and serve.

YELLOW MORNING

28.3% alc/vol
0.7 standard drinks

10ml (¹/₃fl oz) Banana Liqueur
10ml (¹/₃fl oz) Peter Heering Liqueur
10ml (¹/₃fl oz) Cognac

Layer ingredients in order given into a cordial embassy glass and serve.

E.T.

BANANA BOMBER

21.9% alc/vol
0.6 standard drinks

15ml (½fl oz) Banana Liqueur
15ml (½fl oz) Triple Sec
3 dashes Grenadine

Pour ingredients into a cocktail shaker over ice and shake. Strain into a chilled shot glass and serve.

ORANGE

PASSION JUICE

16.2% alc/vol
0.6 standard drinks

20ml (²/₃fl oz) Orange Curaçao
10ml (¹/₃fl oz) Cherry Brandy
15ml (½fl oz) Fresh Orange Juice

Layer ingredients in order given into a shot glass and serve.

OKANAGAN

23.6% alc/vol
0.6 standard drinks

10ml (¹/₃fl oz) Blue Curaçao
15ml (½fl oz) Strawberry Liqueur
5ml (¹/₆fl oz) Coconut Liqueur

Layer ingredients in order given into a cordial embassy glass and serve.

Okanagan

SKITTLE BOMB

6.6% alc/vol
0.9 standard drinks

30ml (1fl oz) Cointreau
150ml (5fl oz) Red Bull

Pour cointreau into a shot glass then place into a highball glass. Add red bull by pouring gently into highball glass around shot glass and serve.

CITY HOT SHOT

16.7% alc/vol
0.3 standard drinks

8ml (¼fl oz) Triple Sec
8ml (¼fl oz) Blue Curaçao
8ml (¼fl oz) Grenadine

Pour ingredients in order given into a cordial embassy glass – do not stir, then serve.

Skittle Bomb

SMURF TOWN

16.5% alc/vol
0.5 standard drinks

15ml (½fl oz) Blue Curaçao
15ml (½fl oz) Peach Schnapps
5 drops Grenadine
Fresh Whipped Cream (chilled)

Pour curaçao and schnapps into a shot glass. Stir and float cream on top.
Add grenadine by drops over cream and serve.

WHITE HOUSE SHOT

24% alc/vol
1 standard drink

30ml (1fl oz) Orange Curaçao
15ml (½fl oz) White Tequila
4 Wedges of Lime

Pour curaçao and tequila into a cocktail shaker over ice then add wedges
of lime. Shake well and strain into two chilled shot glasses then serve.

Smurf Town

WINDY

15.5% alc/vol
0.5 standard drinks

10ml (1/3fl oz) Blue Curaçao
10ml (1/3fl oz) Vodka
10ml (1/3fl oz) Pineapple Juice
10ml (1/3fl oz) Sweet and Sour Mix

Pour ingredients into a cocktail shaker over ice and shake. Strain into
a chilled shot glass and serve.

HIROSHIMA BOMBER

23% alc/vol
0.6 standard drinks

23ml (¾fl oz) Triple Sec
8ml (¼fl oz) Bailey's Irish Cream
3 drops Grenadine

Pour triple sec into a shot glass and layer bailey's on top. Add grenadine
by pouring drops into centre of drink and serve.

Hiroshima Bomber

BAZOOKA JOE

29.3% alc/vol
0.7 standard drinks

10ml (^{1}/₃fl oz) Blue Curaçao
10ml (^{1}/₃fl oz) Grand Marnier
10ml (^{1}/₃fl oz) Banana Liqueur

Pour ingredients in order given into a shot glass – do not stir, then serve.

NECROPHILIAC

21.5% alc/vol
0.5 standard drinks

15ml (½fl oz) Blue Curaçao
15ml (½fl oz) Advocaat

Layer ingredients in order given into a cordial embassy glass and serve.

Necrophiliac

PURPLE VW

16.7% alc/vol
0.4 standard drinks

20ml (²/₃fl oz) Blue Curaçao
10ml (¹/₃fl oz) Grenadine

Pour ingredients into a shot glass, stir well and serve.

BONONO

29.3% alc/vol
1 standard drink

15ml (½fl oz) Triple Sec
15ml (½fl oz) Grand Marnier
15ml (½fl oz) Banana Liqueur

Layer ingredients in order given into a tall dutch cordial glass and serve.

SOUTHERN COMFORT
& WHISKY

BLOOD CLOT

18.5% alc/vol
0.9 standard drinks

30ml (1fl oz) Southern Comfort
15ml (½fl oz) Grenadine
15ml (½fl oz) Lemonade

Pour grenadine into a chilled old-fashioned glass and add lemonade. Stir gently and add southern comfort – do not stir, then serve.

TRIPLE IRISH SHOOTER

32.4% alc/vol
0.8 standard drinks

10ml ($^1/_3$fl oz) Irish Whiskey
10ml ($^1/_3$fl oz) Irish Mist
10ml ($^1/_3$fl oz) Bailey's Irish Cream

Layer ingredients in order given into a cordial embassy glass and serve.

Blood Clot

GREAT WHITE SHARK

37.8% alc/vol
0.9 standard drinks

15ml (½fl oz) Tennessee Whiskey
15ml (½fl oz) White Tequila
Dash Tabasco Sauce

Pour ingredients into a cocktail shaker over ice and shake. Strain into a chilled shot glass and serve.

SOUTHERN FRUITY PASSION

20.6% alc/vol
0.6 standard drinks

12ml (²/₅fl oz) Southern Comfort
12ml (²/₅fl oz) Triple Sec
12ml (²/₅fl oz) Grenadine

Pour grenadine into a cordial embassy glass and layer southern comfort on top. Layer triple sec on top and serve.

Southern Fruity Passion

EARTHQUAKE SHOOTER

34.3% alc/vol
0.8 standard drinks

10ml ($^1/_3$fl oz) Southern Comfort
10ml ($^1/_3$fl oz) Amaretto
10ml ($^1/_3$fl oz) Sambuca

Layer ingredients in order given into a cordial embassy glass and serve.

BLOODY CHICKEN

40.7% alc/vol
1.5 standard drinks

30ml (1fl oz) Wild Turkey Bourbon
15ml (½fl oz) Tequila
Drop of Tabasco Sauce

Pour bourbon into a shot glass and add tequila – do not stir. Add sauce and serve.

Earthquake Shooter

GREEN APPLE

30.4% alc/vol
1 standard drink

30ml (1fl oz) Southern Comfort
5ml (¹/₆fl oz) Midori
5ml (¹/₆fl oz) Sweet and Sour Mix

Pour ingredients into a mixing glass over ice and stir. Strain into a chilled shot glass and serve.

BLACK KENTUCKY

39.4% alc/vol
1.4 standard drinks

30ml (1fl oz) Blended Whiskey
15ml (½fl oz) Black Sambuca

Pour sambuca into a shot glass and layer whisky on top then serve.

Green Apple

PROTEIN SMOOTHIE

13.3% alc/vol
0.3 standard drinks

10ml (1/3fl oz) Scotch Whisky
10ml (1/3fl oz) Clamato Juice
10ml (1/3fl oz) Fresh Cream (chilled)

Pour ingredients into a cocktail shaker over ice and shake. Strain into
a chilled shot glass and serve.

ALABAMA SLAMMER SP
STYLE SHOOTER

14.6% alc/vol
1.2 standard drinks

30ml (1fl oz) Southern Comfort
15ml (½fl oz) Amaretto
60ml (2fl oz) Cranberry Juice

Pour ingredients into a cocktail shaker over ice and shake. Strain into three
chilled shot glasses and serve.

URBAN COWBOY

38.9% alc/vol
1.4 standard drinks

15ml (½fl oz) Southern Comfort
15ml (½fl oz) Grand Marnier
15ml (½fl oz) Tennessee Whiskey

Pour ingredients in order given into a shot glass – do not stir, then serve.

SOUTHERN BONDAGE

20.9% alc/vol
0.7 standard drinks

8ml (¼fl oz) Southern Comfort
8ml (¼fl oz) Amaretto
8ml (¼fl oz) Peach Schnapps
8ml (¼fl oz) Triple Sec
5ml ($^1/_6$fl oz) Cranberry Juice
5ml ($^1/_6$fl oz) Sweet and Sour Mix

Pour ingredients into a cocktail shaker over ice and shake. Strain into a chilled shot glass and serve.

SWEATY IRISHMAN

29.1% alc/vol
0.7 standard drinks

15ml (½fl oz) Irish Whiskey
15ml (½fl oz) Cinnamon Schnapps
Dash of Tabasco Sauce

Pour ingredients in order given into a shot glass – do not stir, then serve.

CRÈME DE CACAO
& CRÈME DE MENTHE

RACE WAR

25.7% alc/vol
0.9 standard drinks

15ml (½fl oz) Dark Crème De Cacao
15ml (½fl oz) Bailey's Irish Cream
15ml (½fl oz) Vodka

Layer ingredients in order given into a tall dutch cordial glass and serve.

FIFTH AVENUE

15.3% alc/vol
0.5 standard drinks

15ml (½fl oz) Dark Crème De Cacao
15ml (½fl oz) Apricot Brandy
15ml (½fl oz) Fresh Cream (chilled)

Layer ingredients in order given into a cordial lexington glass and serve.

Fifth Avenue

SPRINGBOK

18.5% alc/vol
0.5 standard drinks

23ml (¾fl oz) Green Crème De Menthe
8ml (¼fl oz) Amarula Cream
5ml (⅙fl oz) Fresh Cream (chilled)

Layer ingredients in order given into a cordial embassy glass and serve.

MARIJUANA MILKSHAKE

14.7% alc/vol
0.5 standard drinks

15ml (½fl oz) White Crème De Cacao
15ml (½fl oz) Midori
15ml (½fl oz) Fresh Milk (chilled)

Pour ingredients in order given gently into a shot glass – do not stir, then serve.

GERMAN CHOCOLATE CAKE

19.5% alc/vol
0.6 standard drinks

15ml (½fl oz) Dark Crème De Cacao
15ml (½fl oz) Malibu
5ml (1/6fl oz) Frangelico
5ml (1/6fl oz) Fresh Cream (chilled)

Pour ingredients into a cocktail shaker over ice and shake. Strain into a chilled shot glass and serve.

CREAM HASH

24% alc/vol
0.9 standard drinks

20ml (2/3fl oz) Dark Crème De Cacao
20ml (2/3fl oz) Dark Rum
Fresh Whipped Cream (chilled)

Pour ingredients into a shot glass and stir. Float cream on top and serve.

CHOCOLATE CHIMP

24.1% alc/vol
0.9 standard drinks

15ml (½fl oz) Dark Crème De Cacao
15ml (½fl oz) Tia Maria
15ml (½fl oz) Banana Liqueur

Layer ingredients in order given into a tall dutch cordial glass and serve.

MINT CHOCOLATE

20.7% alc/vol
0.5 standard drinks

15ml (½fl oz) Green Crème De Menthe
8ml (¼fl oz) Bailey's Irish Cream
8ml (¼fl oz) Kahlúa

Pour ingredients into a shot glass, stir and serve.

Chocolate Chimp

ANGEL'S RIDE

20% alc/vol
0.7 standard drinks

15ml (½fl oz) Dark Crème De Cacao
15ml (½fl oz) Brandy
15ml (½fl oz) Fresh Cream (chilled)

Layer ingredients in order given into a pousse café glass and serve.

THE KOOCH

20% alc/vol
0.5 standard drinks

15ml (½fl oz) Dark Crème De Cacao
15ml (½fl oz) Bailey's Irish Cream
Cinnamon

Pour cacao and bailey's into a shot glass – do not stir. Sprinkle cinnamon
on top and serve.

Angel's Ride

POOL SHOOTER

27.1% alc/vol
0.7 standard drinks

10ml (1/3fl oz) Dark Crème De Cacao
10ml (1/3fl oz) Green Crème De Menthe
10ml (1/3fl oz) Brandy
Dash Advocaat
Dash Cherry Advocaat

Layer first three ingredients in order given into a cordial embassy glass
and add advocaats individually by drops. Allow these drops to be
suspended half way down the drink for visual effect and serve.
This shooter was created by the author of this book.

Pool Shooter

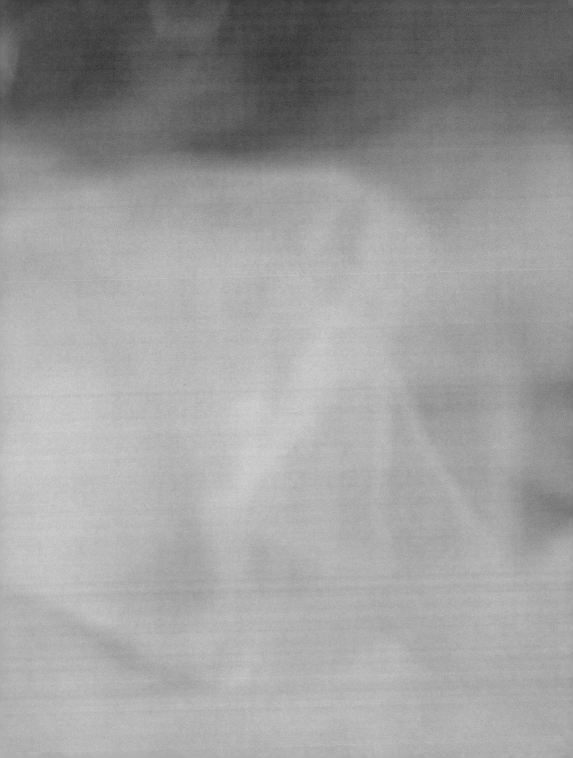

CHAMBORD
& JÄGERMEISTER

G-SPOT

17.8% alc/vol
0.6 standard drinks

15ml (½fl oz) Chambord
15ml (½fl oz) Southern Comfort
15ml (½fl oz) Fresh Orange Juice

Pour ingredients into a cocktail shaker over ice and shake. Strain into
a chilled shot glass and serve.

MIND PROBE

49.5% alc/vol
1.2 standard drinks

10ml ($^{1}/_{3}$fl oz) Jägermeister
10ml ($^{1}/_{3}$fl oz) Sambuca
10ml ($^{1}/_{3}$fl oz) 151-Proof Rum

Pour ingredients in order given into a shot glass – do not stir, then serve.

G-Spot

LIQUID COCAINE SHOOTER

51.3% alc/vol
1.8 standard drinks

15ml (½fl oz) Jägermeister
15ml (½fl oz) 151-Proof Rum
15ml (½fl oz) Goldschläger

Layer ingredients in order given into a tall dutch cordial glass and serve.

SEX ON THE BEACH SHOOTER

12.5% alc/vol
0.3 standard drinks

10ml (¹/₃fl oz) Chambord
10ml (¹/₃fl oz) Midori
10ml (¹/₃fl oz) Pineapple Juice

Pour ingredients into a cocktail shaker over ice and shake. Strain into a chilled shot glass and serve.

Sex On The Beach Shooter

NAZI SURFER

26% alc/vol
0.9 standard drinks

23ml (¾fl oz) Jägermeister
15ml (½fl oz) Malibu
5ml (1/6fl oz) Pineapple Juice

Pour ingredients into a mixing glass over ice and stir. Strain into a chilled
shot glass and serve.

BIKINI LINE

26.6% alc/vol
0.6 standard drinks

10ml (1/3fl oz) Chambord
10ml (1/3fl oz) Tia Maria
10ml (1/3fl oz) Vodka

Pour ingredients into a cocktail shaker over ice and shake. Strain into
a chilled shot glass and serve.

JAGER BARREL

18.4% alc/vol
0.4 standard drinks

10ml (¹/₃fl oz) Jägermeister
10ml (¹/₃fl oz) Root Beer Schnapps
10ml (¹/₃fl oz) Cola

Pour jägermeister and schnapps into a mixing glass over ice. Stir and strain into a chilled shot glass. Add cola, stir gently and serve.

TERMINATOR

36% alc/vol
1.1 standard drinks

20ml (²/₃fl oz) Jägermeister
20ml (²/₃fl oz) Southern Comfort

Pour ingredients into a cocktail shaker over ice and shake. Strain into a chilled shot glass and serve.

BLOOD OF SATAN

39.7% alc/vol
1.3 standard drinks

10ml (¹/₃fl oz) Jägermeister
10ml (¹/₃fl oz) Goldschläger
10ml (¹/₃fl oz) Irish Whiskey
10ml (¹/₃fl oz) Tennessee Whiskey

Layer ingredients in order given into a tall dutch cordial glass and serve.
This drink is also known as Red Cross.

BERLIN WALL

42.9% alc/vol
1 standard drink

10ml (¹/₃fl oz) Jägermeister
10ml (¹/₃fl oz) Goldschläger
10ml (¹/₃fl oz) Rumplemintz

Layer ingredients in order given into a cordial embassy glass and serve.

RED CROSS

39.7% alc/vol
1.3 standard drinks

This drink is also known as Blood Of Satan – page 158.

BRUISED HEART

18.4% alc/vol
0.9 standard drinks

15ml (½fl oz) Chambord
15ml (½fl oz) Peach Schnapps
15ml (½fl oz) Vodka
15ml (½fl oz) Cranberry Juice

Pour ingredients into a cocktail shaker over ice and shake. Strain into
a chilled large shot glass and serve.

COCAINE

17.8% alc/vol
0.6 standard drinks

15ml (½fl oz) Chambord
15ml (½fl oz) Vodka
15ml (½fl oz) Grapefruit Juice

Pour ingredients into a cocktail shaker over ice and shake. Strain into a chilled shot glass and serve.

GALLIANO & SAMBUCA

FLATLINER

37.1% alc/vol
1.2 standard drinks

20ml (²/₃fl oz) Sambuca
Dash Tabasco Sauce
20ml (²/₃fl oz) White Tequila

Layer ingredients in order given into a cordial lexington glass and serve.

KING'S CUP

22.8% alc/vol
0.4 standard drinks

15ml (½fl oz) Galliano
8ml (¼fl oz) Fresh Cream (chilled)

Layer ingredients in order given into a cordial embassy glass and serve.

King's Cup

WARM LEATHERETTE

28.3% alc/vol
0.7 standard drinks

15ml (½fl oz) Black Sambuca
10ml (1/3fl oz) Amaretto
5ml (1/6fl oz) Grenadine

Pour sambuca into a cordial embassy glass and layer amaretto on top.
Add grenadine by pouring down inside rim of glass and allow to settle
on bottom of drink then serve.

SIMPSON BRONCO

24.8% alc/vol
0.9 standard drinks

30ml (1fl oz) Sambuca
8ml (¼fl oz) Grenadine
8ml (¼fl oz) Fresh Orange Juice

Pour ingredients into a mixing glass over ice and stir. Strain into a chilled
shot glass and serve.

Warm Leatherette

IRISH WIDOW

33.6% alc/vol
1 standard drink

30ml (1fl oz) Sambuca
8ml (¼fl oz) Bailey's Irish Cream

Layer ingredients in order given into a cordial lexington glass and serve.

SATAN'S MOUTHWASH

39% alc/vol
0.9 standard drinks

15ml (½fl oz) Sambuca
15ml (½fl oz) Tennessee Whiskey

Pour ingredients into a shot glass, stir and serve.

BLACK RAIN

18.7% alc/vol
0.5 standard drinks

8ml (¼fl oz) Black Sambuca
23ml (¾fl oz) Champagne

Pour ingredients in order given into a shot glass, stir briefly and serve.

BUDDINS

24.1% alc/vol
0.6 standard drinks

10ml (1/3fl oz) Galliano
10ml (1/3fl oz) Bailey's Irish Cream
10ml (1/3fl oz) Butterscotch Schnapps

Layer ingredients in order given into a cordial embassy glass and serve.

CAMEL DRIVER

27.5% alc/vol
0.9 standard drinks

20ml (2/3fl oz) Sambuca
20ml (2/3fl oz) Bailey's Irish Cream

Layer ingredients in order given into a cordial lexington glass and serve.
This drink is also known as Dirty Nipple.

Buddins

DIRTY NIPPLE

27.5% alc/vol
0.9 standard drinks

This drink is also known as Camel Driver – page 168.

DC-3

26.1% alc/vol
0.6 standard drinks

10ml (¹/₃fl oz) Sambuca
10ml (¹/₃fl oz) Bailey's Irish Cream
10ml (¹/₃fl oz) White Crème De Cacao

Layer ingredients in order given into a cordial embassy glass and serve.

DC-3

URINE SAMPLE

31% alc/vol
0.7 standard drinks

10ml (1/3fl oz) Galliano
10ml (1/3fl oz) Midori
10ml (1/3fl oz) Vodka

Pour ingredients into a mixing glass over ice and stir. Strain into a chilled shot glass and serve.

VARIOUS

SWELL SEX

20.7% alc/vol
0.6 standard drinks

10ml (¹/₃fl oz) Malibu
10ml (¹/₃fl oz) Midori
10ml (¹/₃fl oz) Vodka
5ml (¹/₆fl oz) Pineapple Juice
½ teaspoon Fresh Cream (chilled)

Pour ingredients into a cocktail shaker over ice and shake. Strain into
a chilled shot glass and serve.

A.B.C.

50.8% alc/vol
1.8 standard drinks

15ml (½fl oz) Absinthe
15ml (½fl oz) Bacardi
15ml (½fl oz) Green Charteuse

Layer ingredients in order given into a tall dutch cordial glass and serve.

Swell Sex

MUSHROOM

12.7% alc/vol
0.5 standard drinks

15ml (½fl oz) Grenadine
15ml (½fl oz) Midori
15ml (½fl oz) Bailey's Irish Cream

Pour grenadine into a shot glass and layer midori on top. Add bailey's by pouring into centre of drink – do not stir, then serve.

POUSSE L'AMOUR

30% alc/vol
1.4 standard drinks

15ml (½fl oz) Maraschino Liqueur
Yolk of 1 Egg (unbroken)
15ml (½fl oz) Bénédictine
15ml (½fl oz) Cognac

Layer ingredients in order given into a pousse café glass and serve.

Mushroom

ARE YOU TOUGH ENOUGH?

14.2% alc/vol
2.9 standard drinks

15ml (½fl oz) Rumplemintz
15ml (½fl oz) Aftershock
15ml (½fl oz) 100-Proof Scotch Whisky
15ml (½fl oz) 100-Proof Tequila
15ml (½fl oz) 100-Proof Vodka
180ml (6fl oz) Soda

Pour rumplemintz, aftershock, whisky, tequila and vodka into a mixing glass over large amount of ice. Stir vigorously until cold and strain into a chilled old-fashioned glass. Drink as a shooter with a glass of desired soda as a chaser.

JUICY FRUIT

21.6% alc/vol
0.5 standard drinks

15ml (½fl oz) Raspberry Liqueur
8ml (¼fl oz) Triple Sec
8ml (¼fl oz) Midori

Pour ingredients in order given into a shot glass – do not stir, then serve.

ALICE FROM DALLAS SHOOTER

32.7% alc/vol
1.2 standard drinks

15ml (½fl oz) Mandarine Napoleon
15ml (½fl oz) Kahlúa
15ml (½fl oz) Gold Tequila

Layer ingredients in order given into a shot glass and serve.

GILA MONSTER

24.4% alc/vol
0.6 standard drinks

10ml (1/3fl oz) Fresh Orange Juice
10ml (1/3fl oz) Jägermeister
10ml (1/3fl oz) Gold Tequila

Layer ingredients in order given into a cordial Embassy glass and serve.

MEXICAN CHICKEN

15% alc/vol
0.9 standard drinks

30ml (1fl oz) Tequila
Dash Tabasco Sauce
1 Fresh Egg

Pour egg into a liqueur glass and add tequila – do not stir. Add sauce and serve.

FLAME THROWER

30.9% alc/vol
0.8 standard drinks

8ml (¼fl oz) Brandy
8ml (¼fl oz) Bénédictine
15ml (½fl oz) White Crème De Cacao

Layer ingredients in order given into a shot glass and serve.

Mexican Chicken

SCREAMER

35% alc/vol
1.1 standard drinks

8ml (¼fl oz) Gin
8ml (¼fl oz) Light Rum
8ml (¼fl oz) Tequila
8ml (¼fl oz) Triple Sec
8ml (¼fl oz) Vodka

Pour ingredients into a mixing glass over ice and stir. Strain into a chilled shot glass and serve.

OYSTER SHOT

36.8% alc/vol
0.9 standard drinks

30ml (1fl oz) Tequila
Dash Tabasco Sauce
1 Fresh Oyster

Place oyster into a shot glass and add tequila. Add sauce – do not stir, then serve.

KAMIKAZE

21% alc/vol
0.7 standard drinks

15ml (½fl oz) Tequila
15ml (½fl oz) Triple Sec
15ml (½fl oz) Fresh Lime Juice

Pour ingredients into a cocktail shaker over ice and shake. Strain into a chilled shot glass and serve.

STREETCAR

21% alc/vol
0.5 standard drinks

10ml (⅓fl oz) Apricot Brandy
10ml (⅓fl oz) Dark Crème De Cacao
10ml (⅓fl oz) Bailey's Irish Cream

Layer ingredients in order given into a cordial embassy glass and serve.

GRAND-MA IN A WHEELCHAIR

26.2% alc/vol
0.9 standard drinks

20ml (²/₃fl oz) Grand Marnier
10ml (¹/₃fl oz) Tequila
5ml (¹/₆fl oz) Fresh Lime Juice
10ml (¹/₃fl oz) Lemon-Lime Soda

Pour grand marnier, tequila and juice into a cocktail shaker over ice. Shake and strain into a chilled shot glass. Add soda, stir gently and serve.

BAD STING

27% alc/vol
0.7 standard drinks

8ml (¼fl oz) Grenadine
8ml (¼fl oz) Anisette
8ml (¼fl oz) Grand Marnier
8ml (¼fl oz) Tequila

Layer ingredients in order given into a cordial lexington glass and serve.

PLEASURE DOME

33.3% alc/vol
1.2 standard drinks

15ml (½fl oz) Brandy
15ml (½fl oz) White Crème De Cacao
15ml (½fl oz) Bénédictine

Layer ingredients in order given into a tall dutch cordial glass and serve.

VOLVO

36% alc/vol
1.1 standard drinks

8ml (¼fl oz) Apricot Brandy
8ml (¼fl oz) Cognac
8ml (¼fl oz) Cointreau
8ml (¼fl oz) Grand Marnier
8ml (¼fl oz) Vodka

Pour ingredients into a shot glass, stir and serve.

RAGING INDIAN

28.8% alc/vol
0.7 standard drinks

8ml (¼fl oz) Everclear
8ml (¼fl oz) Kahlúa
8ml (¼fl oz) Fresh Orange Juice
8ml (¼fl oz) Mango Nectar

Pour ingredients into a cocktail shaker over ice and shake. Strain into a chilled shot glass and serve.

GREAT BALLS OF FIRE

28.9% alc/vol
1 standard drink

15ml (½fl oz) Goldschläger
15ml (½fl oz) Cinnamon Schnapps
15ml (½fl oz) Cherry Brandy

Layer ingredients in order given into a shot glass and serve.

PASSED OUT NAKED ON THE BATHROOM FLOOR

49.7% alc/vol
1.3 standard drinks

8ml (¼fl oz) Rumplemintz
8ml (¼fl oz) Jägermeister
8ml (¼fl oz) Gold Tequila
8ml (¼fl oz) 151-Proof Bacardi

Pour ingredients in order given into a shot glass – do not stir, then serve.

NUTTY IRISH

20.5% alc/vol
0.5 standard drinks

15ml (½fl oz) Frangelico
15ml (½fl oz) Bailey's Irish Cream

Layer ingredients in order given into a cordial embassy glass and serve.

WATER-BUBBA

20.3% alc/vol
0.6 standard drinks

15ml (½fl oz) Cherry Advocaat
10ml ($^1/_3$fl oz) Advocaat
12ml ($^2/_5$fl oz) Blue Curaçao

Layer ingredients in order given into a cordial lexington glass and serve.

AGWA BOMB

15% alc/vol
0.7 standard drinks

30ml (1fl oz) Agwa
30ml (1fl oz) Red Bull

Pour red bull gently into a shot glass and layer agwa on top then serve.

Water-Bubba

FOURTH OF JULY

8.3% alc/vol
0.3 standard drinks

15ml (½fl oz) Grenadine
15ml (½fl oz) Fresh Cream (chilled)
15ml (½fl oz) Blue Curaçao

Layer ingredients in order given into a tall dutch cordial glass and serve.

ABSINTHE BOMB

10% alc/vol
1.4 standard drinks

30ml (1fl oz) Absinthe
150ml (5fl oz) Red Bull

Pour absinthe into a shot glass and place into a highball glass. Add red bull by pouring gently into glass around shot glass and serve.

Fourth Of July

THE GIRL MOM WARNED YOU ABOUT

21.8% alc/vol
0.7 standard drinks

8ml (¼fl oz) Grenadine
8ml (¼fl oz) Triple Sec
8ml (¼fl oz) Light Rum
8ml (¼fl oz) Midori
8ml (¼fl oz) Blue Curaçao

Layer ingredients in order given into a tall dutch cordial glass and serve.

STRAWBERRY LIPS

15.3% alc/vol
0.5 standard drinks

15ml (½fl oz) Strawberry Liqueur
15ml (½fl oz) Coconut Liqueur
15ml (½fl oz) Fresh Cream (chilled)

Pour ingredients into a cocktail shaker over ice and shake. Strain into a chilled shot glass and serve.

The Girl Mom Warned You About

BRASS BALLS

20% alc/vol
0.5 standard drinks

10ml (^{1}/$_3$fl oz) Grand Marnier
10ml (^{1}/$_3$fl oz) Peach Schnapps
10ml (^{1}/$_3$fl oz) Pineapple Juice

Pour ingredients into a mixing glass over ice and stir. Strain into a chilled shot glass and serve.

IRONLUNG

38.4% alc/vol
1.2 standard drinks

30ml (1fl oz) Yukon Jack
3 drops 151-Proof Bacardi
Fresh Whipped Cream (chilled)

Pour yukon jack into a shot glass and add bacardi by drops – do not stir. Float cream on top and serve.

GLOSSARY

	% alc/vol	
Absinthe	60	Very dry bitter spirit produced from aniseed, licorice,fennel,hyssop and wormwood. Pernod can be used as a substitute in cocktails.
Advocaat	18	Dutch brandy-based liqueur produced from egg yolk and sugar.
Aftershock	40	Cinnamon-flavour liqueur schnapps.
Agwa	30	Amsterdam herbal liquor produced with Bolivian coca leaf. Also includes 36 botanicals and herbs.
Amaretto	28	Almond-flavour liqueur that originated from Italy in 1525.
Amarula Cream	17	Liqueur cream distilled from marula fruit and was first produced in South Africa in 1989.
Anisette	30	Colourless aniseed-flavour liqueur.
Apricot Brandy	23	Apricot-flavour brandy.
Arrack	45	Distilled spirit from rice wine.
Bacardi	37.5	Brand name of a light rum produced in Cuba.

Bailey's Irish Cream	17	Brand name of a slight chocolate-flavour Irish cream liqueur produced with a blend of Irish whiskey and cream.
Banana Liqueur	23	Banana-flavour liqueur.
Bénédictine (D.O.M)	40	Cognac-based sweet herb-flavour liqueur originally created in 1510 by the Benedictine monks, making it one of the world's oldest liqueurs.
Bourbon	40	Sweet whiskey distilled from corn and produced in America.
Brandy	37	Distilled spirit fermented from grapes. If other fruits are used it must be stated on the bottle's label.
Chambord	16.5	Black raspberry-flavour liqueur produced in the Burgundy region of France.
Champagne	12	Sparkling wine that is produced in the Champagne region of France.
Chartreuse (Yellow)	40	Herbal liqueur produced in France and available in two varieties: yellow – this is light and green – which has a higher % alc/vol at 55% alc/vol.
(Green)	55	
Cherry Advocaat	18	Morello cherry-flavour advocaat.
Cherry Brandy	23	Cherry-flavour brandy.
Coconut Liqueur	23	Coconut-flavour liqueur with a light rum-base.

Cognac	40	Fine brandy produced in France, no other country is permitted to label their brandy as cognac.
Cointreau	40	Sweet orange-flavour liqueur that is colourless and arguably the world's finest triple sec. It has been produced by the Cointreau family in France since 1849.
Crème De Cacao	23	Chocolate and vanilla-flavour liqueur produced from cocoa beans, vanilla and spices. It is available in two varieties: dark and white (clear).
Crème De Menthe	23	Peppermint-flavour liqueur produced in three varieties: green, red and white (clear).
Curaçao	25	Sweet orange-flavour liqueur produced from curaçao orange peel. It is available in six varieties: blue, green, orange, red, white (clear) and yellow.
Drambuie	40	Scotch whisky-based liqueur flavoured from heather honey and herbs.
Everclear	95	Pure grain alcohol spirit that is also available at 75% alc/vol – % alc/vol for recipes containing this spirit have been calculated at 95% alc/vol.
Frangelico	24	Hazelnut-flavour liqueur created by a monk over three hundred years ago in the Piedmont region of Italy.

Galliano	35	Aniseed and licorice-flavour liqueur with a distinctive yellow colour. Produced in Italy from over 80 berries, herbs and roots.
Gin	37	Colourless spirit produced from juniper berries and other botanicals. Gin is the most widely required spirit in cocktails.
Goldschläger	43.5	Clear cinnamon-flavour schnapps liqueur containing 24K gold flakes combined with the spirit.
Grand Marnier	40	Orange-flavour Cognac-based liqueur produced in France and created in 1880. It is available in two varieties: red ribbon and yellow ribbon – red ribbon has a higher % alc/vol at 40% alc/vol.
Grenadine	Nil	Sweet red syrup flavoured with pomegranate juice.
Irish Mist	40	Irish whiskey-based liqueur flavoured with herbs and honey.
Jägermeister	35	Herb liqueur produced in Germany from 56 herbs, fruits and roots. Originally created in 1934 by Curt Mast and the recipe still remains a secret.
Kahlúa	20	Coffee-flavour liqueur produced in Mexico.
Licor 43	31	Vanilla-flavour liqueur produced in Spain from 43 herbs.

Malibu	21	Coconut-flavour liqueur with a light Jamaica rum-base. This sweet clear liqueur is produced in Barbados.
Mandarine Napoleon	40	Mandarin-flavour Belgian liqueur with a Cognac-base and is produced from mandarin (tangerine) peels.
Maraschino Liqueur	40	Cherry-flavour clear liqueur that originated in Italy.
Midori	21	Brand name of a honeydew melon-flavour liqueur that is green in colour and produced by the Suntory Distilling Company in Japan.
Ouzo	37	Aniseed-flavour spirit distilled from anise seeds, berries, herbs and pressed grapes. This spirit was originally produced in Greece.
Parfait Amour	23	Citrus and rose scented, violet colour liqueur. Produced from brandy, citrus and herbs it originated from France.
Pepper Vodka	40	Vodka that is flavoured with red peppers.
Peter Heering	21.8	Cherry-flavour dark red liqueur produced in Holland and was created by Peter Heering in the early 1800s.
Raspberry Liqueur	20	Raspberry-flavour liqueur.
Rum	37	Spirit distilled from sugar cane syrup. There are many varieties of rum worldwide.

Rum (Dark)	37	Spirit is aged in wooden barrels for between three and twelve years with the addition of caramel added in some cases to darken the spirit. Dark rum varieties include Jamaica, Haiti and Martinique rums.
Rum (Light)	38	Spirit aged for approximately six to twelve months in oak casks after being distilled in a column-still which produces clear spirit. Originally produced in the southern Caribbean Islands.
Rumplemintz	50	Peppermint-flavour Schnapps produced in Germany.
Sambuca	38	Aniseed-flavour liqueur produced from aniseed, herbs and roots. This liqueur is produced in Italy.
Schnapps	20	Generic name for flavoured alcohol that is produced from grain or potato mash. Schnapps can be very sweet through to dry with many varieties available – % alc/vol content varies between the varieties. 20% alc/vol is average for commercial schnapps.
Sloe Gin	26	Sweet gin-based liqueur that is flavoured with sloe plums (blackthorn plums).
Southern Comfort	37	Peach-flavour liqueur that is brandy and bourbon-based. Created by M.W. Heron in New Orleans over one hundred years ago.
Spiced Rum	35	Blended with a variety of spices.

Strawberry Liqueur	23	Strawberry-flavour liqueur.
Tequila	38	Spirit distilled from the sap of the dessert dwelling agave plant in Mexico.
Tia Maria	26.5	Coffee-flavour rum-based Jamaican liqueur.
Triple Sec	25	Orange-flavour liqueur produced from orange peel – also referred to as curaçao.
Vanilla Liqueur	20	Vanilla-flavour liqueur.
Vermouth (Dry)	18	A fortified wine-based apéritif produced from herbs, flowers and roots.
(Sweet)	15	
Vodka	37	Clear, odourless and tasteless spirit distilled from fermented grain mash and filtered through charcoal. Traditional Russian and Polish vodkas have subtle aromas and flavours.
Whisky	40	Spirit distilled from grain and then aged. They are produced in blends and single malts.
Wild Turkey	43.4	Brand name of a Kentucky bourbon.
Yukon Jack	50	Brand name of a sweet herb liqueur produced in Canada

INDEX